A DIAMOND IN THE ROUGH

GORDON BOSTIC

Primix Publishing
East Brunswick Office Evolution
1 Tower Center Boulevard, Ste 1510
East Brunswick, NJ 08816
www.primixpublishing.com
Phone: 1-800-538-5788

© 2025 Gordon Bostic. All rights reserved.

No part of this book may be reproduced, stored in a retrieval system, or transmitted by any means without the written permission of the author.

Published by Primix Publishing: 01/24/2025

ISBN: 979-8-88703-426-3(sc)
ISBN: 979-8-88703-427-0(e)

Library of Congress Control Number: 2024917445

Any people depicted in stock imagery provided by iStock are models, and such images are being used for illustrative purposes only.

Certain stock imagery © iStock.

Because of the dynamic nature of the Internet, any web addresses or links contained in this book may have changed since publication and may no longer be valid. The views expressed in this work are solely those of the author and do not necessarily reflect the views of the publisher, and the publisher hereby disclaims any responsibility for them.

CONTENTS

His State of Life 6
The Great Outdoors 7
How They Broke the News 8
Camp Diamond 9
Sunday 10
    At First Sight 11
    Dropped Off 12
    First Night 14
    Orientation 16
    After Dinner 17
Monday 18
    He Passed Her By 19
    The Nature Hike 20
    The Master Prankster 22
    A Lost Afternoon 23
    Melinda 24
Tuesday 25
    Keeping a Low Profile 26
    Old News 27
    The Archery Lesson 28
    Little Success 29
    Putting Him through Hell 30
    The Snipe Hunt 31
Wednesday 33
    Acceptance 34
    Fitting In 35
    The Canoe Trip 36
    Pining Away 39

    The Boys in Cabin E 40
    The Meeting 41

Thursday 43
    Elle's Bunkmates 44
    The Cliques 45
    The Rainy Day 46
    The Nighttime Tales 47
    A Brilliant Flash of Light 48

Friday 49
    Paint Ball 50
    The Two who ate Alone 53
    The Target 55
    Humiliation Nothing New 56
    A Diamond in the Rough 58
    A Prank Gone Awry 60

Saturday 62
    Free Day 63
    Never Knowing Love Before 65
    The Panther 66

Sunday 68
    Sunday Services 69
    The Volleyball Game 70
    The Surprise in the Cabin 71
    Revenge 72
    The Training Course 73

Monday 74
    The Boy from Cabin B 75
    The Vigil 76
    The Scavenger Hunt 77
    A Lack of Trust 79
    The Bear 81

Tuesday 83
    The Campout 84
    Underneath the Stars 86
    A Lack of Energy 87
    The Thunderstorm 88

- Wednesday 90
  - Discovery 91
  - The Rumors.. 92
  - The Altercation 93
  - Reflection 94
  - The Aftermath 95
  - Judgment Already Made 97
  - A New Found Hero 100
- Thursday 101
  - Gone Too Far 102
  - The Camp Director 106
- Friday.. 107
  - One Final Time 108
  - No Wish to Leave... 109
  - Who was this Boy? 110
  - What Love Sometimes Brings 111
  - Epilog... 112

HIS STATE OF LIFE

At school he had been ostracized
As kids would call him names.
He much preferred his own bedroom
Where he could play his games.

For him, friendships were difficult
So, he had ceased to try.
The other kids had thought him weird
For he was very shy.

The older kids had bullied him
But he refused to cry.
Though that only encouraged them
Where harder they would try.

At lunch he always ate alone
And pretty much ignored.
Unless someone bumped into him
Because they had been bored.

He found the highlight of the day
Was when the last bell rung
And he could take his leave of them
As though from prison sprung.

This was the state of life he knew
Where comfort was not shown.
Where all compassion was withheld
As if it was unknown.

THE GREAT OUTDOORS

He never liked the great outdoors
And it no love for him.
For by it he was victimized
To go out on a limb.

He'd visited the park but twice
To find it had no charm.
As he'd slipped off the monkey bars
And had broken his arm.

The other time he was bee stung
When he went down the slide.
A nest was hidden underneath
That no one else had spied.

He had no use for the outdoors
With danger ev'rywhere.
He found it safer in his room
With no threats he's aware.

HOW THEY BROKE THE NEWS

At dinnertime they broke the news
That had been a surprise.
Come summer he would spend two weeks
Where he could exercise.

Although his protests were ignored,
As he knew they would be,
He racked his brain for an excuse
That from this he'd be free.

He was a diamond in the rough
Or so, his parents prayed.
He'd lock himself inside his room
And that was where he stayed.

He'd no social interactions
Nor friends of any kind.
His life was one of loneliness
Which he'd not seemed to mind.

His shyness was a detriment
To what he could become.
But little effort had he made
To shyness overcome.

He needed to be socialized
And camp's the perfect place
Where he could not just hide away
But life be forced to face.

CAMP DIAMOND

Camp Diamond was the one they chose
Whose motto had rung true.
"They'd take a diamond in the rough
And help its light shine through."

His parents felt there's more to him
Than he would dare to show.
And this camp may be the outlet
That would help him to grow.

They worried he's afraid of life
Where risks he would not take.
Like he feared the repercussions
Of making a mistake.

They knew he lacked self-confidence
Which he'd need to acquire.
For life is sometimes difficult
And skills he would require.

 # SUNDAY

AT FIRST SIGHT

The camp, it seemed, had been immense
When first it came in view.
And it was built upon a lake
Whose water was deep blue.

There were rows and rows of cabins
That spaciously were spaced.
And with three much larger buildings
That towards the lake had faced.

There was a stream and waterfall
That fed into the lake.
And the whole place was surrounded
With woods that showed no break.

Most would see it as idyllic.
To him it looked like hell.
There appeared to be no wifi
As far as he could tell.

DROPPED OFF

The moment they had pulled away
He felt alone and scared.
It seemed to him the other kids
Just looked at him and stared.

He feared that this experience
No different than school.
Where he's the butt of ev'ry joke
Cause they'd not found him cool.

He knew that he would not stand out
Because he never had.
For two weeks here he would be trapped
Which almost made him mad.

But if school taught him anything
It was how to survive.
He only prayed the time passed quick
Till his parents arrive.

A woman then walked up to him
Presenting a huge smile.
She said she was his councilor
And fun things she'd compile.

The woman said her name was Jan
Who'd help him in his stay.
If there was something he should need
She'd not be far away.

Jan then took him to his cabin,
Which had been Cabin A,
And introduced him to his mates
Who all would share his stay.

Their stories had been similar
Which to them had seemed strange.
The four of them would be bunkmates
As though fate would arrange.

His bunkmates felt the same as him
With names Jon, Ben and Kyle.
They, too, had felt like prisoners
As this was not their style.

The three of them were much like him
And all caught out of place.
It seemed that they were losers too
Which they'd no wish to face.

None of the three had wished to come
But all three had been made.
Their parents thought it good for them
Which each had found clichéd.

All three of them were city born,
Exactly as was he
And all had hated the outdoors
But from here could not flee.

FIRST NIGHT

They went to dinner as a group
As they were all they knew.
Some campers had been veterans
But each of them was new.

The Mess Hall had been pretty cool
With its variety.
Though tables were arranged like school
Which sparked bad memory.

He saw her from across the room
The moment he walked in.
It seemed that she was popular
Just judging by her grin.

Her table was completely full
And laughter seemed to reign.
Already they were settled in
And that was clearly plain.

Brad's bunkmates noticed that he stared
And quickly scanned the room
To see what he was staring at
So, breathing could resume.

He thought she had a pretty face
And really liked her smile.
He wanted to walk up to her
But courage too fragile.

Ben suggested he approach her
At least, to ask her name.
There surely was no harm in it
As that seemed pretty tame.

ORIENTATION

After dinner was a meeting
Called orientation.
Where all's attention was required
With no invitation.

They introduced each councilor
And then set forth the rules.
They told them where they're not to go
And not to eat toadstools.

Each morning they're to make their beds
And keep their cabin clean.
They should not wander off alone
And not throw the cuisine.

Devices they would confiscate
As here they were obscene.
And there's no fraternization
Unless both could be seen.

AFTER DINNER

After dinner there were campfires
With all free to enjoy.
There were some where they told stories.
Some music they'd employ.

He wandered by each one of them
To see if she was there.
Though when, finally, he found her
To approach, he'd not dare.

Instead, he felt a sense of guilt
That maybe he's insane.
For it seemed he'd been stalking her
Which he could not explain.

So, he returned to his cabin
To lock himself away.
Perhaps the courage he could find
If given one more day.

Kyle was lying in the darkness
When Brad had stumbled in.
And said to Brad, her name is Elle
But could not see him grin.

 # MONDAY

HE PASSED HER BY

He saw her standing by the lake
When first had come the dawn.
His desire was to approach her
But, instead, just walked on.

He'd nothing much to offer her
As he's not in her class.
He was the lowest of the low
Who many thought an ass.

His heart had ached to talk to her
But he'd not take the chance.
He'd seen that she was popular
And he's not worth a glance.

So, he had simply passed her by
As though some place to be.
But, truth be told, what he had wished
He had ignored, sadly.

THE NATURE HIKE

On the first day after breakfast
The whole camp took a hike.
Jan told them she was confident
They'd see something they'd like.

A chance to commune with nature
Up personal and close.
Where they'd come to see the beauty
Was truly no mythos.

While Jan had kept a steady pace
The four had lagged behind.
Although they stayed upon the trail
They had been walking blind.

Then Kyle said he saw something move
In the brush up ahead.
Immediately the four froze
As if they all were dead.

They saw it as it had emerged
And stepped onto the trail.
Ben said he thought it was a cat
Though had a bushy tail.

Jon moved as though to pet the thing
Which was a huge mistake.
As the damn thing seemed to spray them
Before it made its break.

The smell was truly horrible
And caused their eyes to burn.
They ran around like maniacs
Till Jan came to return.

Unthinkingly she had approached
But then had pulled up short.
She did not have to get too close
To know what they'd report.

She tried her best to ease the smell
Though found little success.
That night they made them sit apart
From all the rest at mess.

Then after lights had been turned off
All four of them agreed
If they were ever to survive
Some help they'd surely need.

Though day one was a disaster
They'd barely gotten through.
Where now they had hoped to God for
Better things in day two.

THE MASTER PRANKSTER

Most of the councilors were great
But then there had been him.
Who proved to be a real hard ass
Whose name, they said, was Tim.

He never had been satisfied
With anything they did.
It was never to his standards
But underneath had slid.

His sense of humor had seemed sick
To any with a soul.
For he was a master prankster
Who sometimes lost control.

It seemed he found enjoyable;
Though no one could say why,
When the pranks he orchestrated
Had made his victims cry.

He'd received numerous warnings
His pranks he must desist.
But each he'd chosen to ignore
As though he can't resist.

A LOST AFTERNOON

The afternoon completely spent
In dealing with the smell.
Jan tried some homemade remedies
But they had not worked well.

The nurse from the infirmary
Had shared a thought or two
But neither one had proved to work
Admitting failure too.

The stigma, now, that followed them
Was really hard to take.
The four of them were city bred
Who just made a mistake.

Thank God they grew oblivious
To how bad was the smell.
Although all the other campers
Had failed to fare as well.

MELINDA

Melinda had the biggest boobs
Of any girl in camp.
Which she used to her advantage
The way she'd preen and vamp.

She drew all the guys' attention
And never was alone.
As though she had a master plan
Where each she'd come to own.

The other girls were envious
Of notice she received.
Although some had been suspicious
Of growth she had achieved.

Her bunkmates found her secretive
Each morning when she'd dress.
But when inquiries had been made
It's shyness she'd confess.

Regardless she was popular
And rarely seen alone.
If there's a secret she concealed
No sign of it was shown.

TUESDAY

KEEPING A LOW PROFILE

At breakfast they had still been shunned
They hoped because of smell.
They had ignored the snide remarks
Behind their backs they'd yell.

They'd barely been there one full day
And they'd been set apart.
They were the butt of all the jokes
As if none had a heart.

It clearly had been evident
That a mistake was made.
But it was not intentional
To warrant this cascade.

The four agreed what they must do
Was keep a low profile.
Whatever challenge they may face
They must not fail the trial.

OLD NEWS

It appeared their skunk encounter
Already was old news.
It seemed Melinda stuffed her bra
And now must pay her dues.

The flag pole had presented it
As it was on display
With tissues taped inside of it
As a dead giveaway.

Melinda had been mortified
Her secret was revealed.
She wanted to be popular
So, secret she concealed.

She did not show her face for days
So great had been her shame.
She only wished she knew the one
Who for this she could blame.

THE ARCHERY LESSON

Each morning brought activities
But afternoons were free.
There were a host of things to do
Though some thought too many.

He tried his hand at archery
To find he was no good.
The instructor tried to help him
The best he thought he could.

But Brad was not a natural
Although he really tried.
A dozen arrows he had shot
And all had gone way wide.

There almost was an accident
Which had cost him his bow.
Brad swore the arrow merely slipped
But how, he did not know.

Brad's explanation was suspect.
His teacher less than thrilled.
For his teacher had suspicioned
Brad may have wished him killed.

So, Brad was banned from archery
And each activity
Which had involved pointy objects
They judged to be deadly.

LITTLE SUCCESS

At dinner they had all bemoaned
Not one of them had found
One single damn activity
That they could be around.

While Ben had chosen pottery
The object that he made
Had brought his teacher near to tears
As though she was afraid.

Then Jon had said he tried wood burning
Till he had burned his hand.
So, it was the infirmary
He finally would land.

Brad told them of the archery
Where he had been misled.
By accident he let one fly
But missed the teacher's head.

Then Kyle had been the last to speak
As though he was ashamed.
For he'd signed up for cooking class
And for the fire was blamed.

Next Ben had said he'd one more thing
And may need their assist.
His teacher scheduled him to see
The camp psychologist.

PUTTING HIM THROUGH HELL

Ben thought it was ridiculous
The way Brad pined for Elle.
Ben constantly was prodding him
But all to no avail.

But from his perch upon the shore
Ben watched it all unfold.
It could be she was teasing him
And, if so, thought it cold

Although she had been with a group
It seemed to Ben she knew
That Brad was closely watching her
Through ev'rything she'd do.

And though she seemed to be relaxed
Ben really could not tell
If it had been intentional
That she'd put Brad through hell.

THE SNIPE HUNT

That night the councilors had said
That there would be a hunt.
The first year campers were the ones
Who're meant to bear the brunt.

They said the hunt may take all night
With snipe a clever thing.
The rest of camp would beat the brush
While they'd catch those who'd spring.

They handed each a stick and bag
And said to be alert.
A snipe could be quite dangerous
When danger they'd assert.

They loaded all the snipe catchers
Into a pickup truck.
Then drove them deep into the woods
Where they were dropped and stuck.

Now they were stranded in the woods
It's Kyle who thought to ask.
How would a snipe they recognize
To even do this task?

A skunk they misidentified
And paid a heavy price.
They had no clue what was a snipe
So, they'd just roll the dice.

Ben said that they were given bags
Into which they must fit.
So, anything that matched that size
They must assume was it.

Jon marveled as the sun came up
That they had not seen one.
To hear the tales there should have been
At least, you'd think, a ton.

When they, at last, returned to camp
It's to resounding cheers.
The hunt had been a great success
As they're now seen as peers.

WEDNESDAY

ACCEPTANCE

Good natured ribbing greeted them
When breakfast time arrived.
How dangerous had been the hunt
They luckily survived.

A warm feeling swept over him
That he'd not known before.
For it seemed Brad was accepted
Not one they would ignore.

It seemed the smelly incident
Had long since been forgot.
Where now he had been one of them
And subject to their lot.

The ribbing he found he enjoyed
When he was not the butt.
This time he was a part of it
And joke had been clear-cut.

FITTING IN

It seemed by lunch the smell had dulled
Though most had still recoiled.
They heard the snickers when they'd pass
That something must have spoiled.

They agreed in the afternoon
They'd all try something new.
Each choosing an activity
They thought that they could do.

At dinner they would compare notes
Of their experience.
There must be something here to do
That to them made some sense.

They now possessed a single goal
That had, yet, to begin.
Something they'd not do normally
And that was to fit in.

THE CANOE TRIP

The morning's camp activity,
In something called canoes,
Would be a crossing of the lake
To see the far side views.

It had been clear right from the start
The boys from Cabin A
Had not possessed a single clue
How to get underway.

For both canoes had capsized twice
But both times close to shore.
Then Kyle smacked Brad with a paddle
He forgot was an oar.

Although they never mastered it
They showed they'd some control.
And so, the party had set out
To undertake their goal.

Then for some reason that's not clear
They reeked of confidence
And they began to clown around
Which truly made no sense.

Jon stood as though he's Washington
Crossing the Delaware.
The boat abruptly overturned
With Jon flung in the air.

Ben tried his best to right the boat
But had found no success.
Then noticed Jon was not with him
Which almost brought sickness.

While Brad and Kyle were of no help
As their canoe would stall.
They both paddled like maniacs
But went nowhere at all.

Ben called for Jon, but no response
Had he heard in return.
He scanned the waters of the lake
But no form could discern.

But then he heard a muffled moan
Behind the upturned boat.
A paddle hit Jon in the head
So, he struggled to float.

The other campers all had paused
To watch the spectacle.
Then saw it may be serious
Not just an obstacle.

The other campers turned around
And paddled to their aid.
The situation serious
Or so, they were afraid.

Two boys helped Jan to right the boat
And Jon they got inside.
Then Jan and Ben rowed back to shore.
The rest behind them plied.

They took Jon to his second home,
Which was infirmary,
The moment they returned to shore
To halt catastrophe.

Ben addressed the other campers
And had apologized
That they had ruined their outing
When their canoe capsized.

They'd seen the panic for themselves
That had been on display.
And thus, there'd been no snide remarks
Just thanks they were okay.

PINING AWAY

Each afternoon there was free time
Where all enjoyed the lake.
Although there were shenanigans
No rules they'd ever break.

Brad was floating in the water
When Elle approached the lake.
He thought she was so beautiful
A breath he could not take.

As she slipped into the water
He could not help but think
She had seemed to be so perfect
That from her he would shrink.

Most likely she'd think him a dweeb
Just like the rest in camp.
The story had been all the rage
They'd even sometimes ramp.

Although he had, yet, to meet her
He still had been afraid
That when once she got to know him
She'd find mistake was made.

THE BOYS IN CABIN E

The boys from Cabin E were jerks
Who thought they owned the camp.
They were nothing more than bullies
With tempers quick to ramp.

They were the largest boys in camp
And thought that they were crowned.
The councilors had no control
To whom they'd push around.

At meals they'd dare to jump the line
Though few protests were made.
For it was clear that all in camp
Had of them been afraid.

They loved to see the young ones run
So great had been their fear.
Their goal was to intimidate
And did so with a sneer.

It's rare that one would challenge them
By getting in their way.
They were a pack of animals
Who're always seeking prey.

The boys in Cabin A had seen
What damage they could do.
So, they had done the best they could
To stay out of their view.

THE MEETING

The sunset brought Brad solitude
Where sometimes he'd lament
The times he'd locked himself away
Had not been time well spent.

But as the sunset turned to dusk
Elle sat down next to him.
She said his friends had cornered her
And thanks he owed to them.

They told her that he wished to meet
But he was very shy.
She thought she'd take initiative
And give it one good try.

His eyes had told her he was shocked
That she'd come up to him.
As though he feared it was a trick
Or dare made on a whim.

She told him that her name was Elle.
He told her he was Brad.
He'd not believed his bunkmates told
Although he had been glad.

She was unlike the other girls
Who'd seemed shallow and vain.
She was a very thoughtful girl
With thoughts she'd entertain.

His time with her had quickly passed
To where it had grown late.
She told him that she had to go
Although their talk was great.

He asked if they could speak again
To which she'd merely smile.
Which had left him in a quand'ry
If yes or denial.

THURSDAY

ELLE'S BUNKMATES

Elle's bunkmates had seemed really nice.
At least, they were polite.
For they joined them at their table
And did not mask the sight.

Although it started awkwardly,
Once ev'ryone relaxed
They ate in pleasant company
With no one overtaxed.

They shared some common interests
Which left them all surprised.
They thought they were from different worlds
But now felt energized.

With dinner done they had paired up
And set off in the night.
Not one of them thought possible
They'd find this much delight.

THE CLIQUES

It took less time than Brad had thought
Before the cliques appeared.
The camp brochures stressed unity
Which long since disappeared.

The tables in the Mess Hall proved
There'd been a great divide.
For ev'ry meal it was the same
Where each one would reside.

The campers seemed to gravitate
Towards those with common likes.
While those who lived outside their clique
Had fostered deep dislikes.

Brad told Ben he hated cliques
Reminding him of school.
Where most had been innocuous
But one or two would rule.

When Ben told Brad they were a clique
It caught Brad by surprise.
He'd never been a part of one
So, to the fact unwise.

THE RAINY DAY

They'd scheduled a scavenger hunt
To be held on day four.
Instead, it had rained cats and dogs
And really seemed to pour.

Most chose to hang out in the lodge
Where, at least, it was dry.
They found there was not much to do
But watch the time slip by.

Then Jan broke out some old board games
From which to pick and choose.
It seemed to be an ancient art
But they'd nothing to lose.

Surprisingly, they found it fun
Which they did not expect.
Which proved that sometimes older things
Deserving of respect.

Since rain had forced them all inside
Dinner they improvised.
Roasting hot dogs in the fireplace
Was something Jan devised.

THE NIGHTTIME TALES

Their councilors were sometimes cruel
With stories they would tell.
There was the legend of the lake
And spirits in the dell.

Some of the guys, especially,
Would spin an awful tale.
Like deep beneath the waterfall
A cave that led to hell.

The younger kids they terrorized
With all their gruesome lore.
Though warned to not be doing it
Those warnings they'd ignore.

Ev'ry cabin had a flashlight
Should come emergencies.
But after nights of hearing tales
They killed the batteries.

A BRILLIANT FLASH OF LIGHT

It was a brilliant flash of light
That woke Brad from his sleep.
He thought, at first, it was a fire
But then said, "What the (bleep)!"

For Jon was naked on his bed
With a lighter in hand.
He'd strike a light and then pass wind
When fire shot as though canned.

At first it was hilarious
Till his sheets caught on fire.
They quickly had extinguished it
Before it had grown dire.

Though worried how they'd explain this,
For someone's sure to ask.
He knew the truth could not be told
As that they'd have to mask.

Then Brad asked what had possessed him
That this should come to mind.
With all the things there were to do
It's this he'd come to find.

FRIDAY

PAINT BALL

It seemed the day's activity
Was chosen just for them.
After all, the four were gamers
Though never knew a gym.

But their games were electronic
Which they had mastered all.
So, the four felt quite confident
They're born to play paint ball.

Though their confidence was shaken
With the helmets and vests.
Then they were handed the paint guns
Which strapped across their chests.

They were divided into teams
That they termed red and blue.
Each team was given their own flag
Which they'd be loyal to.

They were told that their objective,
Capture the other's flag.
Which required both stealth and cunning
If it they were to snag.

The course specifIc'ly designed
To cross rugged terrain.
Which provided lots of cover
But, also, was a pain.

The distance was a quarter mile
From where each team would start.
They told them when the siren sounds
The teams could break apart.

There was no elimination
For those who had been shot.
But if a paint ball was to strike
It really hurt a lot.

Brad mastered Final Fantasy
So, using that approach
He came up with a master plan
That was beyond reproach.

The four of them would draw the fire.
The rest could then outflank.
Which freed the girls from Cabin Five
To grab their flag point-blank.

They'd leave behind a small reserve
That would protect their flag.
Who'd taken strategic cover
So, intruders they'd tag.

Then when they heard the siren sound
They charged across the course.
Brad's plan was now in full effect
As they attacked in force.

They took the brunt of the barrage
That had been sent their way.
While teammates flanked their opponents
And at them fired away.

Their opponents caught in crossfire
Had no place they could go.
The girls from Cabin Five snuck in
Which proved to steal the show.

The siren rang a second time
Which noted end of game.
Brad's team had been victorious
And garnered the acclaim.

There were cheers of jubilation
And also some delight
That Jon, somehow, survived the game
With no wound they could cite.

Though as the celebration waned
Jon slipped and struck his head.
The nurse already was prepared.
"Welcome back." All she said.

THE TWO WHO ATE ALONE

Ben was the first to notice them.
The two who ate alone.
They sat at tables by themselves
Where insults had been thrown

The girl was clearly overweight.
The boy, they said, not right.
Ben felt a sense of empathy
At the familiar sight.

They'd been caught up in their travails
That they were rendered blind
To all outside their circumstance
Whose treatment was unkind.

The others ridiculed the two
Which they had thought not right.
They chose to go and sit with them
Which had not missed Elle's sight.

He told them that his name was Boyd
But little else made sense.
For most of what he verbalized
Had seemed to be nonsense.

The girl's name, she said, was Berta
And she had seemed quite nice.
She had a strange sense of humor
And grammar was precise.

When they all had finished eating
They offered an invite.
Where the two of them could join them
At dinner time that night.

THE TARGET

It seemed that Boyd was targeted
Which Brad had thought unfair.
The boy, clearly, had special needs
Which all had been aware.

The boys from Cabin H no need
Of finding an excuse.
It was for their own amusement
That they doled out abuse.

And Boyd, it seemed, had asked for it
As he's an easy mark.
The boys would simply torment him
To try to light a spark.

Though against his better judgment
Brad dared to intercede.
And told the boys from Cabin H
That Boyd they'd not impede.

They waited till Brad was alone
Before revenge they'd seek.
And when the boys were done with him
They left Brad in a heap.

HUMILIATION NOTHING NEW

Elle couldn't tell if he's embarrassed
Or simply was ashamed.
It looked as though he'd not fought back
So, he, himself, he blamed.

As horrible as it had seemed
Such was his state in life.
His struggles should have made him strong
Instead cut like a knife.

Humiliation nothing new
To someone of his state.
By now he'd come to terms with it
Accepting it's his fate.

She said he can't accept as fact
His life must be this way.
There must be things that he can do
To help him break away.

Elle told him that he must believe
In possibilities.
The life he knew he could escape
Though may face penalties.

Though they all have flaws and virtues
They're basic'ly the same.
Thus, it all comes down to choices
We find the life we claim.

He can't expect to get respect
Until it is he'd learn
That he must first respect himself
Before that tide would turn.

A DIAMOND IN THE ROUGH

He was a diamond in the rough
That could not be refined.
And yet, there's something she had seen
That could not be defined.

He was a diamond in the rough
Which had been plain to see.
But deep inside Elle greatly feared
That's all he'd ever be.

He seemed to lack initiative
As though he was afraid
Any act of self-improvement
Was a choice poorly made.

She could tell he was no coward
But offered no defense
Whenever he had been attacked
Which really made no sense.

His shyness was a detriment
With which he would not deal.
Elle was drawn to his humbleness
Though unsure it was real.

In many ways a paradox
Of promise unfulfilled.
He hid something inside himself
He had not wished revealed.

He suffered the indignities
That had been thrown his way.
And never offered a defense
Though never ran away.

A PRANK GONE AWRY

The lights had barely been turned off
When Kyle had screamed in fear.
There had been something in his bed
He'd no wish to be near.

Then Ben absolutely lost it.
He laughed so hard he cried.
While Kyle had been beside himself
With anger he can't hide.

Kyle demanded that Ben tell him
What it was he had done.
It was his bed that was messed with
And Ben must be the one.

Ben tried his hardest to confess
But he could barely speak.
His laughter almost crippled him
As tears ran down his cheek.

Ben mumbled something … Hershey's bar,
Which really made no sense.
But he kept pointing to the bed
Which also seemed nonsense.

Then Brad handed Kyle the flashlight
As Kyle pulled back the sheet
To find his bed had come alive
As ants were in retreat.

The whole bed was alive with them
After the Hershey's bar.
While all four had stared in horror
At what had seemed bizarre.

The other three then turned to Ben
Who seemed to be in awe.
As though he was incredulous
To see the things he saw.

The other three broke down and laughed
When they had seen Ben's face.
For this was clearly not a plan
That Ben would dare embrace.

It never had been Ben's intent
For this to have occurred.
It seemed his prank had gone awry
And shame he now endured.

SATURDAY

FREE DAY

They called Saturday a free day
To do what they may please.
There were no planned activities
On which the two would seize.

The whole day they'd spend together.
At least, that's what they planned.
But their bunkmates interceded
With plans they thought less grand.

It began with the eight of them
When Kyle had mused a thought
Why not invite Boyd and Berta
And give those two a shot.

Then the group had mulled it over
To finally agree.
For those two, it seemed, were outcasts
As once they used to be.

The day started with a picnic
They shared beside the lake.
Where Brad and Elle had to admit
It was a pleasant break.

Next the whole group had gone swimming
Where passed the afternoon.
Boyd and Berta enjoyed themselves
Though found the end too soon.

At dinner they ate together
Which clearly caused a stir.
For the two the camp deemed losers
When to them they'd refer.

NEVER KNOWING LOVE BEFORE

He never had known love before
So how was he to gage
If the feelings he had for her
Were worthy of their age?

He knew all of the arguments.
For one, they're immature.
As neither had been old enough
To truly feel secure.

And yet, it had seemed real to him
And fairly sure to her.
What they had was something special
While sure she would concur.

Though both were soon to graduate
How could they truly say
If feelings that they felt right now
Would last while worlds away.

THE PANTHER

A group had chose to take a walk
Though it was growing dark.
The camp road seemed the perfect trail
For its outline was stark.

The night presented a full moon
Which helped them clearly view
The path that was laid out for them
Had seemed so fresh and new.

He felt a strange sensation when
Elle had taken his hand.
He had hoped it was affection
He was to understand.

That's when they heard the panther's call
As it was on the prowl.
The sound could make the blood run cold
As like a baby's howl.

A panther can be dangerous
When it was seeking prey.
Brad told the others they should run
While he drew it away.

He stood his ground in wait for it
While all the others ran.
Where for once he was committed
To some form of a plan.

He wondered if he was to die
Would they appreciate
The sacrifice that he had made
While accepting his fate.

The councilors had then appeared
While laughing at their prank.
The campers thought the threat was real
And from it they had shrank.

The courage he displayed that night
Had clearly been ignored.
With focus on the ones who ran
Not he who death implored.

Though Elle was not oblivious
To courage he displayed.
She never dared to mention it
Nor fuss about it made.

SUNDAY

SUNDAY SERVICES

On Sunday they held services
With welcome to extend.
The service they called interfaith
With all free to attend.

Brad knew that Elle had wished to go
So, he said he'd go too.
For all he knew the service crowd
Would only be those two.

He was surprised when they arrived
How many would attend.
He'd never been to church before
So, could not comprehend

What was it that had drawn them here
With so much else to do.
He felt the lake was calling him
But he'd promised Elle too.

He'd never heard the tales before
That morning he had heard.
Where ev'ryone had been the same
Despite a jock or nerd.

And he felt he was uplifted
By everything he'd heard.
Perhaps Elle had known him better
Than ever she'd conferred.

THE VOLLEYBALL GAME

They'd joined a game of volleyball
But none had known the rules.
So, what had been the net result
Was they had looked like fools.

They'd proven they weren't athletes
The way they'd trip and fall.
And half the time they ran around
Losing track of the ball.

The game had quickly drawn a crowd
Who all had been amused.
The way the boys from Cabin A
Had looked dazed and confused.

Though when the game had reached its end
They took a bow or two.
As though with purpose they had staged
A Three Stooges review.

Then they grinned to one another
How quick they came to think
Of the perfect cover story
To hide how bad they'd stink.

THE SURPRISE IN THE CABIN

On day seven after breakfast
They found on their return
A small snake was in their cabin
Which at first brought concern.

Then Ben and Jon both grabbed a broom
To sweep it back outside.
But just as Kyle was entering
Who kicked it back inside.

They used the brooms like hockey sticks
To knock the snake around.
And though it tried to get away
No exit had it found.

Then Jan who had just happened by
Had noticed the ruckus.
And then stopped to investigate
What's the cause of the fuss.

Jan asked them what was going on
Before she grabbed her head.
They thought it was a garter snake
But was a copperhead.

Ben then quickly showed a slap shot
That knocked it out the door.
They told Jan that they were sorry
But, at least, swept the floor.

REVENGE

At mealtime all the councilors
Would all together sit.
If a camper tried to join them
They'd have a royal fit.

T'was Kyle who hatched the basic plan
To which the rest agreed.
They thought it had been payback time
For ev'ry sneaky deed.

They developed little packets
Which they had filled with glue.
That night they snuck into the Mess
With each seat given two.

The next morning when breakfast came,
Completely unaware,
Each councilor had grabbed a seat
And were glued to a chair.

Kyle then burst into the Mess Hall
To claim emergency.
Each councilor leapt to their feet
With chair as company.

The whole Mess Hall then exploded
In laughter and in glee
As the councilors hopped around
While trying to break free.

THE TRAINING COURSE

Brad found the secret training course
The councilors enjoyed.
At night he started slipping out
As it he had employed.

She said that she had faith in him
Which he'd not heard before.
So, he set himself a lofty goal
That he was shooting for.

He found that it was strenuous
But each night he improved,
Though he kept his workouts secret
In fear they'd not approved.

When his bunkmates noticed changes
Brad to them would confess
He knew that he had weaknesses
He swore he would address.

MONDAY

THE BOY FROM CABIN B

There was a boy in Cabin B
They said reckless and wild.
There was no dare he would not take
Especially when riled.

Some friends of his had dared him jump
From top the waterfall.
They thought it may be twenty feet
To water after all.

The boy displayed no sense of fear
As into space he'd leap.
His friends had cheered him in descent
To find it was not deep.

The water barely covered rocks
That sat along the edge.
And they had not been visible
From high up on the ledge.

The paramedics and police
Were both called to the scene.
And ruled it was an accident
As it was unforeseen.

The whole camp felt a state of shock.
Two councilors were fired.
The whole thing was a tragedy
That foolishness inspired.

THE VIGIL

Brad met Elle outside her cabin
But there had been no joy.
They were heading to the vigil
To remember the boy.

The service was a grim affair
Held under candlelight.
Where even those who'd not known him
Would in their grief unite.

It was a rude awakening
To see what had occurred.
They thought they were invincible
But now, not so assured.

The boy ignored what were the rules
And paid the frightful price.
Where now they would be mourning him
For he had tossed the dice.

Although kind words were said of him
The sadness did not fade.
They said he was a daredevil
And for that dearly paid.

THE SCAVENGER HUNT

Tim and Jan called them together
Before the hunt began.
Then divided them into teams
For that had been the plan.

Each team then given a short list
Of twenty things to seek.
With the only true restriction
Three hours were the peak.

Brad wished that Elle was on his team
But that did not occur.
Instead, their goals were opposite
Which he did not prefer.

He had hoped he could stay focused
But found his thoughts consumed
With what it was that Elle would do
If a new suitor loomed.

He found his insecurities
Had left him with self-doubt
That Elle may be too good for him
Which she may figure out.

While he'd been lost in soul-searching
His team had done quite well.
For of the twenty items sought
Nineteen already fell.

There still were fifteen minutes left
And all they'd left to find
Was the feather of an eagle
Which to Brad brought to mind

He knew there was a nesting pair
Down by the waterfall.
His team took off at double time
In race to the rock wall.

A girl from Cabin Three had screamed
The feather she had found.
They'd just begun to celebrate
When heard the siren sound.

But Brad's elation disappeared
As Elle's team had emerged.
Elle was joking with a stranger
As self-doubt reemerged.

Jon thought that he had been immune
But found it was not true.
The poison ivy covered him
Which he'd reacted to.

It was the outcome of the hunt
That they did not expect.
Jon back in the infirmary
So, rash they could correct.

A LACK OF TRUST

Ben had heard Elle's voice in the woods
And stopped to say hello.
He knew how much she'd meant to Brad
And prayed, she too, would know.

But Ben had seen when she emerged
She was with company.
The boy he did not recognize
But they had seemed friendly.

Ben then told Kyle what he had seen
Where Kyle had been surprised.
Kyle never thought Elle was the type
Whose feelings were disguised.

Kyle was appalled Elle would betray
Someone he called a friend.
Though not one for confrontation
But friend he would defend.

Yet, when he had confronted Elle
She truly had seemed shocked.
As she just stood and stared at Kyle
As though she had been mocked.

Kyle said that Ben had seen her with
A boy whose name's not Brad.
Elle said that Ben had been correct
But found it really sad

That there was such a lack of trust
To think she would betray
Someone who meant so much to her
And she'd find that okay.

Not ever knowing friends before
They found trust an issue.
Not only knowing when to trust
But never sure of who.

THE BEAR

The bear had seemed to be a threat
With councilors concerned.
At night it wandered into camp
And trash cans overturned.

It did not seem to be that brave
For if they showed, it ran.
But their concerns were not allayed
As there may be a clan.

But as the days and nights wore on
More brazen it became.
Where the Mess Hall was a target
The bear had grown to claim.

Some councilors chased it away
But it soon came to learn
They would not dare to follow it
So, soon it would return.

They had called some forest rangers
To have the bear removed
With the plan they would sedate it
So, then it could be moved.

As sunset slowly turned to dusk
With ev'ryone in place.
They waited for the bear to come
Where threat they could erase.

They did not have to wait too long
Before it lumbered in.
Then something seemed to startle it
Which caused the bear to spin.

Next Jon had stepped out from the woods
Just as the ranger fired.
The dart completely missed the bear
But Jon the dart acquired.

The second ranger did not miss
So, down had gone the bear.
They said they would relocate it
To somewhere far from there.

They said that Jon would be okay
From lasting injury.
They took him to his favorite place
Which was infirmary.

TUESDAY

THE CAMPOUT

It was strictly voluntary
The overnight campout.
Where they would hike into the woods
And under stars sleep out.

Elle said that she had wished to go
So, of course, Brad went too.
He never had camped out before
So, this was something new.

Brad's bunkmates were not up for it
So, he'd gone on his own.
In hope that he could find some time
To be with Elle alone.

They would be roughing in the wild
Just like the days of yore.
Where they may face some challenges
They'd never faced before.

Each camper brought their own bedroll
Plus, some necessities.
There'd be two meals they must prepare
While living midst the trees.

The trail had climbed up by the falls
And followed by the stream.
Elle took his hand as they had walked
Just as he'd sometimes dream.

Brad was not sure how far they walked
But they had walked a while.
The distance, though, was not so great
That any lost their smile.

They found a glade in which to camp
Not far from the small lake.
Where Jan directed all of them
A campfire they must make.

For dinner they roasted hot dogs
Over an open fire.
Then told stories till the embers
Said it's time to retire.

They spread their bedrolls 'neath the stars
And all had settled in.
Though Brad and Elle had moved away
From where the rest had been.

And while the rest fell fast asleep
Those two remained awake.
For, at last, they'd found solitude
That for which both would ache.

UNDERNEATH THE STARS

They laid there underneath the stars
Though neither said a word.
For fear the moment would be spoiled
If any sound was heard.

He reached for her. She reached for him.
Then silently held hands.
They found true magic in the night
Devoid of love's demands.

He'd not known what had possessed him
That he would take the chance.
But the feeling overwhelmed him
Which was once of romance.

Then he leaned over to kiss her,
Though he had not known how.
But to Elle it made no diff'rence
As all she said was, "Wow."

He watched her as she fell asleep
But kept a watchful eye.
His mission was to keep her safe
Under the starry sky.

A LACK OF ENERGY

Brad was not sure if he had slept
As he watched out for Elle.
If he had slept at any time
He had not slept that well.

However, Elle had looked refreshed
And not the least bit tired.
While he had fought to stay awake
With energy expired.

Elle asked him what the problem was
But Brad would not confess
That sleep would rarely come to him
When he's under duress.

He felt his role was to protect
As he felt they're exposed.
So while he's watching over her
She sweetly had reposed.

She fussed at him the whole way back
For showing lack of pep.
But it was hard to keep the pace
And yawn with ev'ry step.

THE THUNDERSTORM

That night there came a thunderstorm
That had grown quite intense.
The thunder had been deafening
And lightning no pretense.

The thunderstorm grew serious
Where most had grown afraid.
As though the devil beat his wife
For some mistake she made.

The boys in Cabin A awake
As the rain was intense.
It beat upon the cabin's roof
As their only defense.

When in the distance they heard cries
Of panic and alarm.
Though none had wished to go outside
And place themselves at harm.

But Brad had thought he heard Elle's voice
So, volunteered to go.
The storm, it seemed, intensified
As though to tell him, no.

Brad stumbled through the knee-deep mud
Though he could barely see.
But when he reached Elle's cabin door
He saw their misery.

Their roof had partially collapsed
And all four, soaking wet.
They'd tried their best to find refuge
But efforts were not met.

Brad told the four to all hold hands
As he'd taken Elle's hand.
He'd lead them back to his cabin
Where storm they could withstand.

When they arrived, the boys prepared
With blankets, towels and rags.
The five of them had all been drenched
As though they were dishrags.

They then bunked down the best they could
To just ride out the night.
They woke to find the storm was gone
And there was bright sunlight.

WEDNESDAY

DISCOVERY

The councilors were horrified
To find what they had found.
The eight of them had shared the night
While to the cabin bound.

Jan said there could be no excuse
When they tried to explain.
In fact, Jan had grown furious
With thoughts she'd entertain.

Brad had tried to reassure her
That nothing had occurred.
They had merely given shelter
When trouble they incurred.

Brad told Jan just to look at them
As they're covered in mud.
The cabin that had housed the girls
Was subject to a flood.

Jan admonished them to shower
Before to mess they came.
For perhaps a thorough cleaning
Would wash away their shame.

THE RUMORS

The camp, it seemed, was all abuzz
With rumors that weren't true.
The whispers raged behind their backs
Of what they did not do.

The whispers that surrounded them
They weren't supposed to hear.
But all assumed the very worse
And that was very clear.

Their looks could give their thoughts away
As they passed through the room.
The snickers and the snide remarks
They knew would surely loom.

Jan approached them at their table
To say she wished inform
The Director wished to see them
And expect a firestorm.

THE ALTERCATION

The rumors really bothered Brad
As some of them were crude.
Especially the boys from E
Who tended to be rude.

Brad took exception to comments
The boys from E had made.
But when they dared call Elle a slut
Brad's course was clearly laid.

Although outnumbered four to one
Brad did not hesitate.
They goaded him into a fight
And he'd taken the bait.

A small crowd gathered to observe
The beating Brad would take.
But Brad, it seemed, surprised them all
As he struck like a snake.

The altercation had been brief
Though neither side backed down.
There were some punches that were thrown
But Brad proved he's no clown.

REFLECTION

When he returned to his cabin
Brad's bunkmates were aghast.
His face had been a total mess
That they could not get past.

His bunkmates merely stared at him
As though they'd not believed
This was the guy they had bunked with
Who rarely had been peeved.

His face all puffy, scraped and bruised
For reasons he concealed.
His bunkmates' questions he ignored
Despite how they appealed.

He'd no desire to speak of it
And wished to be alone.
He was ashamed of what he'd done
And shame he'd have to own.

He never thought that he could stoop
To depths that were that low.
They goaded him into a fight
And he had not said no.

THE AFTERMATH

Elle looked for Brad when she had heard
The stories passed around.
How Brad had faced the boys from E
And firmly stood his ground.

Elle's face reflected more than shock
When she at last found Brad.
The stories must have all been true
For he looked pretty bad.

When she asked him what had happened
He tried to turn away.
For he was somewhat embarrassed
And not known what to say.

Then she asked him if he's crazy
As she'd already known
All the details of the skirmish
That his face had now shown.

Then she asked him why he did it
As the act seemed so grim.
Why he'd resort to violence
Which had not seemed like him.

It seemed his limits had been breached
For insults he'd let slide.
But he found he could not take it
If she they would deride.

She had then embraced and kissed him
Which caused him to grimace.
It seemed sometimes when she's happy
She could be a menace.

JUDGMENT ALREADY MADE

The Director apoplectic
When he had been informed.
He thought the rules were crystal clear
And had not been reformed.

He told them they should be ashamed
For taking liberties.
They knew the rules that were in place
And still did as they'd please.

Though once again they tried explain
Exactly what occurred.
The Director just looked through them
As though nothing he'd heard.

A judgment was already made
Regardless what was true.
As though he knew in confidence
It's something he would do.

Then he said they're on probation
And with one more offense
He'd have no choice but kick them out
As justice he'd dispense.

It was not fair they were accused
Of what they had not done.
For he possessed no evidence
Thus, proof he had was none.

That's when Brad took an exception
To ev'rything he said.
There was no investigation.
And facts he had misread.

Elle saw a change come over Brad
That she'd not seen before.
He'd shown a sense of confidence
In justice argued for.

The accusations that were made
Had simply not been true.
They merely helped some friends in need
Which decent people do.

There's nothing wrong with what they'd done
And Brad had took offense
The Director would punish them
Without clear evidence.

It would be easy to check out
The story they relayed.
The girls' cabin was evidence
But research was waylaid.

Brad said he'd had enough of this
Where justice was not served.
He'd not accept a punishment
He felt was undeserved.

With all that said, Brad stood to leave
Which drove the man insane.
Brad flaunted his authority
Which Brad made very plain.

At last, it seemed, the gem appeared
That Elle had thought she spied.
As she had stood and followed Brad
With smile she could not hide.

A NEW FOUND HERO

There was a hush when he walked in
That took Brad by surprise.
He had no need to look around
As he could feel their eyes.

It seemed he'd gained some new respect
And even was admired.
For he'd bravely stood up to them
Which most of them desired.

But none found the strength of courage
That Brad it seemed had found.
For all the campers had grown tired
Of being pushed around.

It appeared that Brad's their hero
Who had stood up for them.
While Elle reflected privately
That she had found a gem.

Then the Mess Hall had erupted
With their applause and cheers.
While those from Cabin E were left
To wallow in their jeers.

The boys from E avoided him
As though he was the plague.
Some campers dared to question them
Though answers had been vague

THURSDAY

GONE TOO FAR

They'd heard the rumors all day long
There'd been a prison break.
The councilors were all abuzz
But claimed the rumors fake.

Then told the day's activities
They'd chosen to suspend.
With all restricted to the camp
Which few could comprehend.

The whole camp, it seemed, was locked down
But no one would say why.
The rumor mill worked overtime
On which few would rely.

They all were left to wonder what
The hell was going on.
It's clear there's knowledge they withheld
With some conclusions drawn.

The sirens wailed to sound alarm
The rumors had been true.
The convicts that had broken free
Were there, though hid from view.

They all took refuge in the lodge
As if their last defense.
Though Brad questioned the rationale
As it made little sense.

A DIAMOND IN THE ROUGH

It was pure pandemonium.
Confusion reigned supreme.
Brad thought that he could taste the fear
That bordered on extreme.

There was no info passed along,
Just rumors in the dark.
Some councilors were hostages
So, this was not a lark.

There were reports someone had seen
Tim was lashed to a tree.
He looked as though they tortured him
And seemed in agony.

The councilor of Arts and Crafts
Who had just been released
Said convicts now controlled the camp
And Tim, she claimed, deceased.

She said Tim told them ev'rything
That they had wished to know.
Their plan to take more hostages
They'd force with them to go.

Brad heard the sobs of those who feared
Tonight, was their last night.
And even those who'd shown resolve
Had given in to fright.

Elle then shifted her position
To be closer to Brad.
She had doubted he'd protect her
But he was all she had.

Then Brad noticed that his bunkmates
Also moved next to him.
He told them that he had a plan
Involving most of them.

Brad had found no rhyme nor reason
To how they may react
But all the campers his concern
To where he now must act.

Though not sure how many convicts
Had stood outside the lodge.
They could rush and overwhelm them
While gunfire they could dodge.

Brad told them they should pass the word
To those who'd volunteer
That each of them should arm themselves
And to the doors move near.

Brad found a newfound confidence
That he'd not known before.
Perhaps it was the circumstance
That forced him to explore.

He was a diamond in the rough
That much she'd clearly known.
But now there was a new resolve
That he had never shown.

When Brad had given the signal
It was a human flood
That had launched itself from the lodge
In search of convict's blood.

The convicts had been so surprised
They, literally, froze.
While campers had assaulted them
As a melee arose.

Till Tim had risen from the dead
To try to put a halt
To what had been a wild response
That truly was his fault.

The whole event had been a prank
That had got out of hand.
There were reports of injuries
But none appeared too grand.

Though Jon, it seemed, was once again
In the infirmary.
For it seemed he turned an ankle
On the root of a tree.

THE CAMP DIRECTOR

The camp director was upset
These pranks had gone too far.
Some campers had been traumatized
Because they'd raised the bar.

This one-upmanship had to stop
Before someone was hurt.
These pranks had grown preposterous
Where caution they'd avert.

The councilors he held to blame
As they should be mature.
Instead, they seemed to instigate
What he thought was manure.

The camp director adamant
These pranks would have to cease.
He was terrified that law suits
Would be on the increase.

FRIDAY

ONE FINAL TIME

Their last night had seemed bittersweet
As neither wished to leave.
For here they'd found a comfort zone
Where magic they could weave.

She promised she'd write ev'ryday.
He feared it was a lie.
For once they were away from here
The memories may die.

He was afraid the night they shared
They'd never share again.
For lack of opportunity
Or some slight change within.

Elle said true love knows no borders
That's known as time and space.
And in her heart, she'd always hold
For him a special place.

He kissed her for the final time
And then he said goodbye.
She looked at him one final time
And then began to cry.

Perhaps next year they'd reunite
As he planned to return.
He hoped that she had planned the same
Though that he'd yet to learn.

NO WISH TO LEAVE

He saw his parents by their car
But had no wish to leave.
He'd have to leave his friends behind
Which he could not conceive.

And then, of course, there had been Elle
Who he could not let go.
She'd now become his ev'rything
Which he prayed she would know.

It's not as though he had a choice
For all good things must end.
It's just that he was not prepared
With sadness to contend.

His bunkmates were already gone
And Elle was soon to leave.
This place to him was magical
Yet, he'd get no reprieve.

He'd found someplace where he belonged
And had no wish to leave.
He feared what he'd accomplished here
He'd nowhere else achieve.

Tomorrow just a memory
He prayed would never fade.
For he'd felt blessed to have been here
With good friends that he made.

WHO WAS THIS BOY?

His parents wondered who he was
That they had come to claim.
This surely had not been their son
Although he shared his name.

This boy exuded confidence
Where their son had shown none.
And he had seemed to have made friends
Which theirs had never done.

And when it came to meeting Elle
They both had been amazed.
The girl, they thought, was beautiful
Yet, by their son seemed dazed.

It seemed he knew near all in camp
As most had said goodbye.
It made them wonder who it was
That they were now to eye.

Apparently, their son was gone
Or clearly was replaced.
Because the boy they're taking home
Was someone they'd not faced.

He was a diamond in the rough
Who had been made to shine.
He once had been unpolished stone
That Elle helped to refine.

WHAT LOVE SOMETIMES BRINGS

The texts and phone calls they exchanged
Grew less in frequency.
Until she'd not respond at all
Despite his urgency.

He had no clue what may be wrong.
Perhaps she'd ceased to care.
Whatever problem there had been
He was left unaware.

Love sometimes brings us misery
Yet, love we still pursue.
As though it's a necessity
That we must answer to.

He consciously had tracked the days
Till camp his one concern
And hoped within his heart of hearts
That Elle, too, would return.

EPILOG

The next year Brad returned to camp
But found Elle a no show.
He asked if any heard from her
Though answer always no.

At first, she'd text him ev'ry day
Then trickled till they ceased.
His texts had then drawn no response
As his concern increased.

He thought it clear she's over him
Or found somebody new.
A fact that he must now accept
Though pretty sure he knew.

A sadness had swept over him
For what he knew he'd lost.
The price of loving at his age
Not worthy of the cost.

He saw the girl walking towards him
And noticed she was cute
Though quickly disregarded her
Believing the point moot.

But then the girl walked up to him
And asked if he was Brad.
His friends said he'd like company
Because he was so sad.

A DIAMOND IN THE ROUGH

Brad turned to see his bunkmates smile
Before they turned away.
Brad asked her if she'd like to walk
To which she said okay.

He never knew where Elle had gone
But gratitude applied.
He was a diamond in the rough
That only she had spied.

ABOUT THE AUTHOR

Gordon Bostic was born in West Virginia and grew up in Virginia. A graduate of James Madison University and Fairleigh Dickinson University, he worked as a computer scientist and a software engineer for most of his life. He began writing at a young age as a way of expressing himself, his feelings and his view of the world. Gordon has also had an interest in telling his stories in one way or another. Gordon currently lives on the Jersey Shore with his wife Susan.

www.ingramcontent.com/pod-product-compliance
Ingram Content Group UK Ltd.
Pitfield, Milton Keynes, MK11 3LW, UK
UKHW040904240225
455493UK00001B/202